Creativity
as a
Life Path

JAN GROENEMANN

Balboa Press books may be ordered through booksellers or by contacting:

Balboa Press
A Division of Hay House
1663 Liberty Drive
Bloomington, IN 47403
www.balboapress.com
844-682-1282

ISBN: 979-8-7652-3532-4 (sc)
ISBN: 979-8-7652-3533-1 (e)

Library of Congress Control Number: 2022918446

Print information available on the last page.

Balboa Press rev. date: 01/31/2023

BALBOA.PRESS
A DIVISION OF HAY HOUSE

Foreword

In this treasure of a book, Jan Groenemann invites us on the heroic journey of creativity as a life path. Through inspiring poetry, compelling stories, and creative examples, she demonstrates that creativity awakens us to the realm of the sacred and our most authentic self. Creativity is a practice, and this book provides a generous toolbox of techniques on how to practice creativity with intention, curiosity, playfulness, and magic. Jan's tools are not just based on theory, but on her own practice and process that have led to her becoming an artist of being alive.

Through the beautiful poiesis of our creativity we are led into a wholeness of being. Creativity heals and empowers as it takes us to the edge of wonder and delights us with awe and surprise. It is an adventurous journey that calls us to cross the threshold of our comfort zone and step into expanded possibility and perspective. French artist Henry Matisse was known for saying that creativity is another word for courage. It takes courage to embrace the bittersweet vulnerability of creative living that can feel so raw, wild, and holy.

Jan is a lover of life, wise sage, and spiritual guide, who has mentored many of us on how to consciously choose creativity as a life path. Her life not only exemplifies creative living at its best, but also the importance of forging creative connections and friendships on the artful journey. The creative path is best not traveled alone, for we are all creative sparks of inspiration for one another. Creative presence enables authentic connection.

Jan and I have traveled creativity as a life path for many years now. One of our greatest lessons and revelations on this profound journey of friendship has been how creativity and spirituality are intimately entwined in this spiraling dance we call life. Each helps us cultivate meaning, connects us to mystery, awakens, and enlivens us. Creativity is ultimately an interactive process of spiritual encounter.

So tend your own creative fire and trust your creative longings as you let Jan guide you on this wonderful journey. If you travel far enough along this creative path, you will one day come home to greet your truest self and say a resounding yes!

With you on the journey,
Holly Eden Carson, MA, LPC, LCSW
Psychotherapist, artist, and co-author of
Weaving Ourselves Whole: A Guide for Forming a
Transformational Expressive Arts Circle

The Elder Grove, 30x30, **oil and cold wax (collection of Fred and Maripat Monterubio)**

We are all not only creative but creators. We are constantly making art in how we dress, how we talk, how we garden, cook, dance, sing, how we decorate our homes, and how we think. Art is life.

We can create out of confusion (chaos) or out of conscious intention. But we are always creating. We create with every thought, action, and choice.

The products of creativity are as uniquely varied as the individuals who produce them. Creative expression is what colors our world and makes us each who we are. If I want to know you I've but to look at what you create.

I have chosen a variety of my own creative works to share with you in these pages with the hope you might be encouraged to more fully explore and discover your own unique creative self-expression. By learning to create with conscious intention, you can create a life you love.

It is my hope that by opening up to you, being vulnerable to you, my reader, you might become more vulnerable in sharing with others the beautiful, creative being that is you.

Creating with intention requires vulnerability.

Jan

This book is dedicated to my dear friend, Stanley Vincent Chambers,

who created a big, unique, and adventurous life!

Widening Circles, 24x36, mixed media

I Saw You Today

In the red and yellow canna's profuse blooming,

So late in the season I thought it would not flower,

But within hours after your passing

A bud shot forth on a strong stem.

This morning

In my mourning I talked to you as there

Grew two new yellow flowers,

And you said, "Of course this is from me for you."

And so I knew peace in the silence and the

Shading of the trees near my studio.

Then, turning to a tapping at the glass of my door,

So intent as not to be ignored,

A wild, red-tailed hawk, my totem,

Namesake of my family of origin,

Persistently pecking for my attention—

I knew instantly it was you,

Felt you, heard your laugh,

Your voice joyous:

"See, all that stuff is but annoyance, when

I can fly with the hawk and bloom with the flower."

For Stan (August 10, 1947-July 5, 2021)

Jelly Fish, 11x14, **oil and cold wax on paper**

Pairings

Clouds, so heavy with moisture that they drip, drip,

Slowly slip in as I carefully clip the roses,

Pull a weed here and there,

Stand back to stare as the garden becomes

Less wildish and out of control.

It is my life I trim, my thoughts,

My whim to run or become rooted,

Or wander with the wildness.

Freedom, too, my style, yet I am aware

There must be some bit of pattern,

Some sense of plan.

Sprinkles begin to trail down my scalp.

They pool and spread across my forehead and forearms,

Still I clip, carry, and toss,

Careful of thorns and poison ivy.

The rain begins to fall steadily,

I readily carry my clippers and gloves inside,

Embracing the melancholy

That moves in with the rain.

Contents

***Goddess,* 3'x3' mixed media**

I have called on the Goddess and found her within myself.

(Morgaine le Fay, *The Mists of Avalon,* Marion Zimmer Bradley, 1982)

Creativity as a Life Path

Learning to Create with Intention

Jan Groenemann

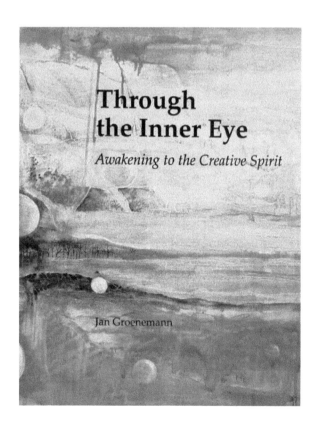

Through the Inner Eye: Awakening to the Creative Spirit by Jan Groenemann was published by Islewest Publishing, Dubuque, IA, 1994.

Creativity as a Life Path is an expansion of the concepts in this book.

A copy of this book is available through Inner Eye Life Coaching or the author. www.jangroenemann.com

Bound copies are limited, but eBooks are readily available.

Acknowledgements

So many have touched my life and inspired me in the years since writing *Through the Inner Eye: Awakening to the Creative Spirit* for which this book is a sequel. I am so grateful to each.

The following have provided valuable support in this most recent endeavor:

My soul sister, Holly Carson, with whom I meet bi-weekly to share on deeply creative and spiritual levels wrote the foreword to both this book and my first. She also edited and gave valuable feedback.

Members of my writer's group: Teddy Norris, Bob Hornbuckle, and Frank Prager served as editors and technical guides.

My daughter-in-law, Renee Groenemann, with whom I am partnering in Inner Eye Life Coaching, along with my son Jason's technical help, are embarking on an exciting journey together with online courses, of which this book is a part, and support for World Changers and Community Weavers. Renee also helped with editing.

My son, Jeremy and daughter-in-law, Meaghan Groenemann have helped me in so many ways both technical and inspirational.

Garic Groenemann, my son, was instrumental in editing both *Woman Alone* and this present book. I'm also excited to share some of his wonderful photography within these pages.

Cortney Tatlow, my niece, has aided in editing both *Woman Alone* and *Creativity as a Life Path*.

Amy Kartmann, Camilla Baxter, Nancy Rickert, and Pat Tait also agreed to read, edit, and give feedback for this book.

I am deeply grateful for the love, support, and validation each of you bring to my life. This book could not have happened without you! Thank you!

Jan Groenemann

The Red Road, 5'x6' mixed media (collection of Camilla Baxter)

The "Red Road" (the Right Path) is a metaphor for living a spiritual way of life. Oglala Sioux traditional healer and holy man, Black Elk, in "Black Elk Speaks," (written by John G. Neihardt) spoke of the people on the red road as being one interconnected circle of people that made a sacred hoop. We each walk our own journey.

Introduction

More than twenty-five years ago, when *Through the Inner Eye: Awakening to the Creative Spirit* was published, I primarily focused on creative expression through the arts, specifically painting and poetry. I had discovered that through my own creative process as a painter and poet I was connected with something more, something beyond my own knowing. It literally seemed that my paintings, for example, knew more than I knew and were teaching me about my surroundings, my relationships, and most of all, my inner self. I realized, through my creative expression, I was being led into a deeper meaning in my life.

At a point when I was going through a very difficult realization about my failing marriage, I came into the studio upset and angry from a confrontation with my now ex-husband. Feeling a need to let out my frustration on paper through painting, I took a large sheet of watercolor paper, wet it with a large brush, and began to drop and throw colors onto the wet paper. I chose reds and purples, working quickly and intensely. The release I felt was fascinating. I found it even more amazing that the anger began to melt away; a feeling of peace came over me. The painting was softening as color melded with the wet paper, and instead of angry blobs of color, there appeared abstracted flowers on a background of soft blues and purples. The message was clear: "Things are happening exactly as they need to." I stared at the finished painting in a surreal calm. I knew it was true. Things were exactly as they needed to be. That very week, *Exactly as It Needs to Be* sold to a client who loved the colors and related to the story of its creation. This seemed to be validation of the truth of its message.

Some achieve great fame; but within, despite achievements, there remains a vague longing for something more.

Each of us needs to believe there is meaning in being here and in going through the process of living that is often difficult and painful. Most of us spend years seeking that meaning outside ourselves through the perfect partner, the perfect job, children, and success. Some achieve great fame; but within, in spite of achievements, there remains a vague longing for something more, as in that old Peggy Lee song, "Is That All There Is?" There is a great deal of joy in finding what constitutes a reason for one's existence. I believe what compels us is what the author, C.S. Lewis, called the "inconsolable longing." Eventually, failing to assuage that longing with our curiosity or our seeking, we are compelled to go within and create from what we find there. It is most surely a longing to know the true Self, the self that sees through the Inner Eye and communes with the Divine.

Photo Study of a Rose

This process clearly opened me to a greater awareness of Self and a deeper sense of my purpose in life. In the twenty-five years since sharing an awakening to this inner guide, not only have those words, *exactly as it needs to be*, proven true, but I've had numerous experiences that equally validate the premise of that first book.

Today many have written about exploring the powerful potential of connecting with one's own creative energy. It seems humans have evolved enough that the time to understand and apply these concepts has come. In her blog for *Psychology Today*, June 6, 2010, Allison Bonds Shapiro, M.B.A. writes, "Dr. Ruth Richards, my friend, and teacher, is fond of reminding me that creativity is our birthright. It is not a special talent limited to famous artists and writers and musicians. We are all creative. We are built to be. Being human requires us to adapt to the changing circumstances of our lives." This is what Dr. Richards, who is certainly an expert on creativity, calls *"everyday creativity."*

After my first book was published, I made creativity my major study as I pursued a Master's Degree in Art and studied in depth what it means to create. I became known as one who specializes in creativity. *Through the Inner Eye* was placed on reading lists for several Art Therapy programs across the United States, and I began facilitating workshops throughout the country. As I continued to share this exciting insight into my own creative self, I found that everyone I worked with, albeit to varying degrees, could connect with and benefit from this inner creative energy. As I observed this magic working in others, it was continually validated for me that creativity is at the very core of who we are, inseparable from our spirituality. Indeed, this may be how we are most like *that from which we come.*

Discovering that exciting creator within not only results in wonderful art and careers based on a sense of purpose, but it makes one's very life more adventurous, more meaningful, and more fulfilling on every level.

Following the inner guidance that was speaking to me through my creative expression, I left a failed marriage and found myself catapulted into the art world determined to make a living doing art. I'd known from the time I was four years old that I wanted to be an artist. And yes, I was teaching private art classes while exhibiting and selling art. But now I was required to make a leap.

I no longer had financial help from a partner; I had to fully support myself as an artist.

Thus began the journey to create a full-time career in art, otherwise, I'd have to go back to teaching art on a secondary level, a position that offered more consistent compensation. I had raised three sons, one with a juvenile diabetes diagnosis at age fourteen months. My art had been put on the back burner and then became a part-time endeavor. Now I had to trust and live the insights I had shared in *Through the Inner Eye*. I had to learn to trust this intuitive inner knowing that was speaking to me through my art and also through my dreams. It had been a combination of the messages I was getting through my creative process and a literal dream that sat me up in the middle of my bed on a Wednesday morning filled with a knowing that I had to get out of my marriage.

As I came to understand more about the creative process, I realized that what some call the *artist's way of seeing* opens us to see all of life on a new level. It affects each of us as a whole person; the creativity inspired by this "seeing" pours over into every aspect of life. Through this "seeing" we are drawn to live life on a deeper, more intimate, and even more spiritual level. I have found it amazing that something so simple as stumbling upon an interesting rock in the middle of my morning walk can, upon really stopping to see it and listen to it, inspire a new painting that once again speaks to me and gives direction concerning my own life situation. Or it may inspire a poem, or a piece of music. This "seeing" isn't just physical, it is spiritual—it opens one to seeing within to that deepest core where every choice, every act becomes a ritual that stretches and grows us.

In this way we come to know life as a blank canvas, or at least a canvas that can be reworked to mirror more closely who we authentically are. I learned I could transform my home, in which I felt "stuck" after divorce, into a nurturing space that gives me rest and inspiration and offers the same to my friends. My garden, too, is another art form. It became a place where I can commune with nature and hear God speak to me daily. Most recently I have created an overnight coaching and creativity intensive that utilizes my garden as a place to renew and enliven clients toward their own creative visions. Even my spiritual practice is a creative adventure in the sense of exploring rituals and interactions that uplift me daily and bring me to moments of bliss. My

business is no longer based solely on teaching art techniques and creating my own paintings. Now it entails training others to connect with their creativity and to make a life they envision for themselves. This includes the exploration of ways of connecting on a deeper level with the inner self, the environment, clients, family, and friends—even the Divine. Every aspect of my life has been impacted by this awareness. Learning to listen to my paintings and poetry as my teachers was a first step that led me to the realization that through this "seeing" everything and everyone becomes my teacher.

My first book was a second step in my awakening. I felt the creative process was alive in me with every breath, and I was compelled to share the excitement of it with others. It led me to dream, to visualize, and to manifest in ways I had not before thought possible, and I wanted others to experience this as well.

A Spiral of Awareness:

In *Through the Inner Eye: Awakening to the Creative Spirit* I began to consider creativity as a *Spiral of Awareness*:

We begin at the bottom by connecting with our **Environment**: the awe-inspiring beauty of nature. From here we move to understand that our **Circumstances** have a powerful effect on us: the culture we are born into, our philosophies and belief systems, the character of our care-givers, etc. As we become more aware, we are shaped deeply by our **Experiences**, both those we choose and those that are part of our **Circumstances**.

Once you start on this path, you will realize that it is impossible to go back. Once you become conscious of the happenings in the world around you, it is not possible for you to become blind to them again, and this is why some might (in extreme moments of course) long for their days of ignorance. In spiritual growth this process is also known by the name of "spiral of awareness."

Unknown

As we continue to grow and become more aware, we begin to care for and make decisions based on the good of **Others.** Here we begin to form deep connections, to touch lives and be touched by **Others**. We seek to assuage our longings all along the way, but **Others** can seem to be the answer as we fall in love and plan to create lives together. Eventually, we are led to look more deeply into the **Self,** so deeply that we discover the Higher Self. We become more authentic and even feel guided. This leads us to an authentic relationship with that ***Creator*** *or source of all creation.*

I have added to **Self** the term **Co-Creator**, because I find it is important to realize one's own creative power that connects us to the **Creator (Divine)**. It is from this point of view we create a vision that leads us to fulfilling work that is from the deepest Self, thriving in our own "Genius Zone." Here we also create relationships that nurture and inspire us. We create a life we want and love—a passion-filled life.

Spirit spreads across the land on the breath of nature, fills our souls and senses, then pours out in our poetry and song.

Through research and experimentation, modern science is coming to the conclusion that conscious observers, meaning you and me, create reality. The more conscious, the more aware we become, the more likely we can create not only a better life for ourselves, but a better world.

Imagination is our ticket for travel to anywhere we want to go!

If indeed it is our consciousness that brings our world around us into reality, then surely we can learn to create that which nurtures and inspires us. We can create a life we love.

This book, a sequel to *Through the Inner Eye: Awakening to the Creative Spirit*, shares parts of my own creative journey with the hope of helping others discover (or further realize) the amazing creative Self that is creating every day and in every aspect of daily life whether from awareness or unawareness.

Becoming aware that every thought we have and every choice we make is a creative action can help us to better focus on those thoughts that are positive and help to create more positive life experiences. It is my wish to share with others how I have come to create, not by accident, but with conscious intention, and how for me creativity has become a conscious life path.

What we perceive as reality is a process that involves our consciousness.

Robert Lanza, M.D.
(The Grand Biocentric Design)

Robert Lanza, M.D., one of the most influential scientists of our time, writes: "The universe bursts into existence from life, not the other way around as we have been taught. For each life there is a universe, its own universe. We generate spheres of reality, individual bubbles of existence. Our planet is comprised of billions of spheres of reality, generated by each individual human and perhaps even by each animal." *(Beyond Biocentrism)*

Creativity is a highly advanced mental process that involves dreaming, imagination, development, and innovation. You are creator of your universe; you are responsible for what you create.

Reflections on the Pond

Detail from Drawn to the Mystery, 4'x 4' Mixed Media

The way I see it is if you want to have the rainbow you have to put up with the rain.

Dolly Parton

Part One

What We Create is a Choice

The most difficult step is the first one you take. Each following step becomes easier. You can do anything you decide to do. You can act to change your life; you can create the life you want.

Amelia Earhart

Maybe if we re-invent whatever our lives give us we find poems.

Naomi Shihab Nye

("Valentine for Ernest Mann," Everything Comes Next)

I recall reading a book in the early 2000's by Frank Minirth, M.D. and Paul Meier, M.D. titled *Happiness is a Choice.* It is a handbook on how to overcome depression; its central thesis is that we are all besieged by events and circumstances that are difficult and depressing, but we have a choice as to how to allow these events and circumstances to affect us. We can see ourselves as victims and bemoan every difficult circumstance, or we can choose to keep (as much as we can muster) a positive attitude and make the best of each situation, even grow and become stronger from it.

The first time I was confronted with my failure to exercise my own power of choice was after spending almost two years in therapy with my husband. Thinking we were repairing our marriage, I was shocked to learn he was still involved in the affair that had sent us into that therapy. Totally distraught, I called our therapist, who could not be reached. Another therapist in the same office took my call. After I explained what was happening she calmly said to me, "Go do something for yourself. Take a long soaking bath, something that takes care of you." I was appalled. What did she mean? Looking back, I fully understand. She was telling me I had a choice. I could continue to base my well-being on the behavior of another, or I could change my focus and do something to take care of me. I wasn't ready to hear this at the time. But now I realize this wise woman had a powerful message for me. I couldn't control what my husband did, but I had a choice as to how I responded to it.

I believe that we do, indeed, have a choice. As I write this, we are more than two years into the nightmare of a worldwide pandemic from COVID-19. In the first couple of weeks, as the reality of what we were dealing with was hitting, I went into deep fear. I especially feared for the welfare of my sons; two with health issues that would make the virus more dangerous for them, and the third works in a large trauma hospital, where he was, in fact, exposed early on.

I quickly realized, however, that this was no way to live. Living in fear meant that I could not fully live my life for worry over "what if." I managed to change my way of thinking. In fact, I chose to be grateful for each day that I awoke healthy and knew my family and friends were healthy. I made the choice, also, to become aware of how living this experience might have something to teach me, our country, and even the world.

So much is happening at this moment in time: the pandemic, political division, civil unrest, school shootings, war, the lack of trust in our leadership and science, and the shakiness of our democracy—I feel it can be no coincidence. We are being challenged to be something more and more authentic.

For years I began my morning with a bike ride of several miles, came back to the studio where I did yoga, then spent fifteen to twenty minutes in meditation before journaling. One morning after finishing this ritual and settling into a comfortable position for meditation, I quickly found myself in an altered state amidst swirling colors. It felt as if I was somewhere out in the universe where I was directly connecting with what I call *Source*. It was a very pleasant experience. In this state I distinctly heard a voice that said, "When you worry about what has happened in the past or what might come in the future, you are not living. Living takes place only in this present moment. Don't miss it. Be present in this now."

What a powerful experience! The visual was so profound that I had to attempt to capture it in a painting, which I eventually did on a 5'x 6' canvas and titled *The Source*. But the message, wow! How very true it is! We only have this moment to live. It was the message of this experience that helped me to stop living the "what ifs" of fear in challenging situations and most recently, the "what ifs" of COVID. Instead, I choose to live in gratitude, moment by moment.

We do have a choice. And each choice we make creates what kind of day we will have and ultimately what kind of life. Most are probably familiar with the line from the Bible, "As a man thinks so is he," (Proverbs 23:7). Our thoughts create, and we are what we create. As a life coach, I have so often seen proof of this fact. If I can help clients shift their way of thinking away from fearful, limiting, and negative, I will quickly see a major change in who they are and how they respond to their circumstances. It is a very exciting process.

When a caterpillar bursts from its cocoon and discovers it has wings, it does not sit idly, hoping to one day turn back. It flies.

Kelseyleigh Reber
(If I Resist)

Teddy social distancing on the deck for a Writer's Group session.

Other writers have thought of this as realizing one's personal power. Creating with intention and trust is our most powerful asset. It is life changing. We can't live this life without difficulties, disappointments, and pain, but we can choose how we will use these things to create the life we want.

My family has, for many years, had a tradition at Christmas of passing a glass lemon to the family member who has experienced the most difficult year. It sits on my bookcase as I write. Last year I suffered almost daily pain from the passing of tiny kidney stones. It took the entire year to learn that this was caused by a medication I was on that was raising my uric acid levels. Within a week and a half of going off that medication I had no more kidney stones. The lemon is to remind us, trite as it may seem, "when life hands you lemons, make lemonade." The lemon is symbolic of the choice to learn all the lessons we can and make the good we can from the tough things life deals us.

Inner Eye Retreat location, New Harmony, IN

By now you may be asking: How do I know I'm making the right choice? This is certainly an important question. Again, I want to remind you that getting to know yourself and connecting with that Authentic Self are keys to making the right choices. This requires some effort and practice. Also, I propose that sometimes there may be no "right choice." One choice simply takes you down a path you might miss if you make a choice that brings different experiences. The point is to trust that you, with sincere effort, will choose what will expose you to the experiences that will best bring you growth as an individual. Sounds like a win/win, doesn't it?

Assuming that you want to feel you are making the best of all possible choices, a good first step for connecting with your inner guidance is the relaxation technique that gets you into "the zone" (explained in the Tools section of this book) for setting intention. It is equally effective when you need to check in when making a choice. Go into the relaxation with the choice you are considering in mind, and ask to have clarity. "The zone" is where you most effectively communicate with your Higher Power. When you come out of the meditative state, go immediately into journaling on the question. Trust what you intuitively feel about the choice once you have finished journaling.

Once you have done the above, if you still feel some confusion or are unsure, talk it over with a wise and trusted friend. Share with your friend your experience during the relaxation/meditation and any thoughts you had while journaling. Simply verbally processing with a friend, or perhaps a life coach, who is a good listener, often clarifies your decision. If not, ask for your friend's gut reaction to what you have shared. Sometimes a friend can pick up on feelings you may not be aware of.

Garden textures.

Finally, if you still feel confused, repeat the relaxation, visualization, and journaling. Remember, also, there are times that you just need to sit with the question a while longer or wait for a sign. Yes, I definitely believe in signs.

Signs are another way our inner guide speaks to us, and I will go into this further in another section. Ultimately you will have to learn to trust your intuitive nudges. I know from experience this takes time and practice, and sometimes it may mean failing to act because you just can't quite trust yourself yet. Be patient.

Creative color and textural choices from *Garic's Garden*, photo by Garic Groenemann

The power of vision is that the moment you determine what your vision is you unconsciously begin to move toward it.

Part Two

Creativity Requires Vision

Your vision will become clear only when you look deep within. Looking without creates frustration; looking within brings awakening.

Carl Jung

Vision is the manner in which one sees or conceives of something. It is a mental image produced by the imagination. We can say, vision is the ability or an instance of great perception, especially of future creations. It is the proven best strategy for creating a life you love. Think of vision as the bigger picture; it defines who you want to be, what you want to be known for, and the set of experiences and accomplishments you aim for. Vision sets the framework for choices and intentions. It is your *why*! Having taken a good number of trips around the sun, I have recreated my own life by setting a new vision several times.

As a small child growing up on a farm I loved my horse, my dog, a yellow, long-haired cat, drawing, painting, and being out in the woods or riding my horse through the fields. My vision was to be an artist, have acreage, horses, dogs, and cats for the rest of my life. A natural romantic, my vision also included falling in love, getting married, and becoming a mom.

As I matured I loved reading, painting, drawing, and learning, so I began to have a vision of going to college and studying art. Of course, I'd still have acreage and animals and be madly in love. As college drew near, I set a vision (though I didn't call it that at the time) to go to college, teach art, create art, and travel the world. I would not get married until I was thirty, then I would have a couple of kids and continue doing what I loved—specifically art. This was the first phase of my life.

Phase two began when I graduated from college and began teaching high school art and intro to business. Within a year, still far from thirty, and before my first summer of travel, I met an amazing, handsome guy and fell madly in love. We married, rode horses, owned a boat, and loved water skiing. I followed him as his engineering work moved him, finding teaching jobs as I could, until I got pregnant with our first child. I kept making art while being a stay-at-home mom and moving five times with my husband's work in the first eight years of our marriage. I was married for twenty-five years. Wife, lover, friend, and mom—creating art as I could manage with three children, seeking to better know myself and God.

Phase three began with divorce. Everything changed. The "Happily Ever After" of my vision evaporated. Disappointment, hurt, and a sense of failure required I rethink everything. I slowly formed a new vision and was catapulted into the art world where I became a real artist—making a living doing art, publishing

True vision allows us to soar higher than we have ever dreamed.

my first book, teaching art, and facilitating workshops on creativity and personal growth. I built a fascinating career. My work was exhibited and sold in galleries throughout the United States and even in Germany, as well as collected in Japan, Belgium, and the UK. The height of this phase found me teaching eighty private students per week out of my home studio; teaching nine hours of Art History, Philosophy, and World Literature in a Humanities cluster at Lindenwood University; and spending twenty-four hours per week as Resident Artist at the Foundry Arts Centre, while still creating art. It was a tough schedule.

Phase four found me envisioning working from a home studio overlooking my Zen garden. I had been in a few relationships, but by now I was very comfortable as a woman alone. Another book was forming in my mind. I had pulled out of most galleries and instead was doing several solo exhibits per year. I wanted to cut back on students and hours in order to have more time to paint and write. When the new studio was finished, I once again stepped into a different world. I left the Foundry and, within three years, also left Lindenwood. I cut the number of classes to four, all held in my home studio, allowing me a slower pace and more time to create.

I now find myself stepping into Phase five. Once again I have set a new vision with new intentions. A pandemic has brought an abrupt halt to my weekly in-studio classes. I am learning new technology and have started doing some classes via Zoom. Also, trained as a life coach, I am working on designing courses for online Webinars and joining my daughter-in-law in Inner Eye Life Coaching, a mostly online venture of courses and coaching to support World Changers and Community Weavers. We hope to work with those who are in the business of helping others to keep a balance in self-care and personal growth. Caregivers need techniques that inspire and nurture them to avoid overwhelm or burnout. My vision includes this same balance for myself, with much time for creating.

We always have a choice. We have the power to break free, clear our vision and create a new life for ourselves.

Even at a very young age I had a vision of being an artist. Thanks to my father, who insisted I get a practical degree, I not only have an undergraduate degree in Art Education, but also in Business where we were taught to set goals. I suppose a goal and a vision have much in common, but I prefer to think of setting your intention on a vision as a bit more organic than a rigid business goal. When you develop a vision for your life you are first looking at the broad, sweeping picture of what you want your life to be. As you take action to move toward creating that vision as a reality, you take small steps, one by one. At any point, as a step takes you nearer to your vision, you may see that you want an adjustment; you may need to tweak that vision. This is what I mean by organic. There is flexibility. Think of a vision as a living thing that may change as you approach it; it is a working plan. Time will help you to see more clearly, so, if needed, you can adjust that vision to better fit with who you are. In fact, your priorities may change as you move toward that vision, which can, in turn, require some changes. Forming a vision then, sets your mind on a direction that you wish to travel.

Before you can effectively create the life you want, you must pin down what that means for you. You must identify what matters to you and put a stake in the ground to work toward. Have a vision, even in the back of your mind, and you will begin to move toward it.

To start forming a vision, sit in a quiet place where you won't be disturbed and think about the different areas of your life. This can include talents, skills, knowledge, character, as well as financial, career, recreation, health, relationships, personal growth and self-care, community, and spirituality. Essentially, a vision helps you define who you want to be and sets a framework for what your life is to look like. Consider also what you have already accomplished, and what makes you feel really inspired and joyful. And, don't forget to dream.

In coaching we use what is called a "life balance wheel" that allows one to consider how much time and priority they want to put into each area of life. I've included a sample of this wheel below to help you begin thinking about your priorities.

Getting wonderful feedback from all across the country with photos from women who had read Woman Alone was even beyond my vision when I was working on the manuscript.

Categories include: Health, Finances, Career/Education, Family, Contribution, Physical Environment, Creativity, Personal Growth, Spirituality, Fun, Intimate Relationships, and Social Relationships. The idea is to decide what percentage of your time and priorities you wish to commit to each category. Draw up your own chart, expanding the color for a category according to how big your priority will be for that area of your life. You can even create your own categories.

It can be helpful to create a life balance wheel for how you see your life right now, and then create a second wheel to show what you would imagine as your perfect balance. For example, at this point in my life, I am adjusting my wheel to allow for more creativity and less career/education as I move away from teaching art classes which once made up a big percentage of my career time.

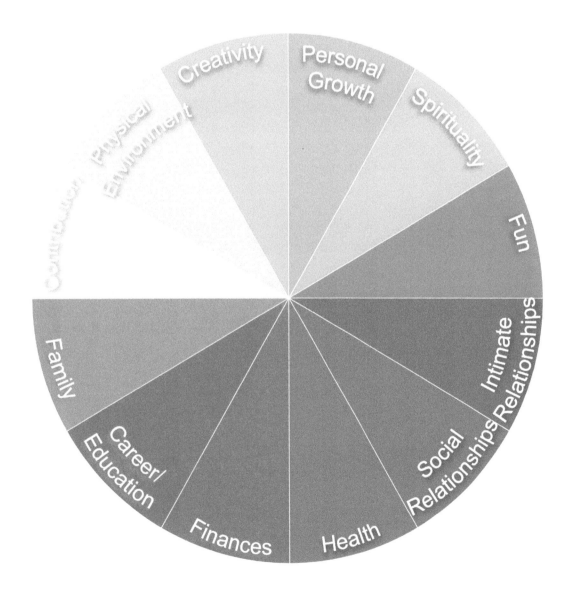

Now, craft a statement of what your ideal life looks like. Write it out trying to be specific. Depending on what age you are, this written statement can answer questions about what life you want to have lived at 20, 30, 40, 50, 60, and so on. It can tell you what kind of people you want to be surrounded by, what you believe you are capable of, what are the greatest things you can accomplish given the right circumstances, what you wish you could change about the world, or contribute to the world that would make you proud and content. When you die what would you like people to say about you? How would you like to be remembered?

No dream is too big, no vision too broad if it is what you feel drawn to do or be. Only you can imagine what is right for you.

Vision is the art of seeing what only you can imagine for yourself.

Determine what percentage of your time and focus you want in each area on the life wheel and write that in. Your vision serves as a compass to help guide you to take the actions and make the choices that propel you toward your best life. It maps out your pathway and gives you your best chance to succeed. If you don't develop your own vision, you'll allow other people and circumstances to direct the course of your life. A life of fulfillment best happens by design. Your vision statement is your design plan.

Here are a few more prompts that might be helpful in forming your vision:

In your vision what will you have accomplished already?
How do you feel about yourself?
What kind of people do you want in your life?
How do you feel about them?
What does your ideal day look like?
Where are you spiritually?
Where do you live? What does your home look like? What state, city, country are you in?
What are you doing?
Are you alone or with a partner, group, team?
How are you dressed?
What really matters to you?
Are you impacting others?
In what way?

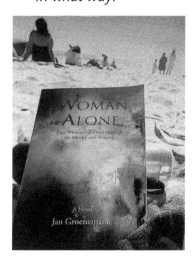 

Left photo is taken on the beach in California by a reader of Woman Alone. Right photo is from a reader in Maryland. How inspiring to have these wonderful photos taken and shared with words of appreciation for the message of Woman Alone.

Izzy's Butterfly, 12x12, mixed media

Belonging to the Universe, mixed media (collection of Sandy Alford)

Part Three

Intention Guides Creativity

Our intention creates our reality.

Wayne Dyer

Setting an intention begins us moving toward our dreams. It is the creative power that fuels our journey toward actualization.

Intention is defined as a thing intended, an action or a plan. An intention correlates to a short-term goal in a business plan. In relationship to your vision, an intention is a step that takes you closer to that vision. Think of vision as what you are moving toward and intention as the movement on the path you are taking to get there. When you set a vision for your life, you are first looking at the broad, sweeping picture of what you want your life to be. As you take action to move toward creating that vision as a reality, you take small steps, one by one. At any point, as a step takes you nearer to your vision, you may see that you need an adjustment. You may want to tweak that vision. A vision is a living thing that may change as you approach it. Time may help you to see more clearly, so that you can adjust that vision to better fit with who you are. In fact, you may change as you move toward that vision, which may also require some changes. Such changes can require a change in intention.

Setting an intention then, forms the stepping stones on the path that you walk, step by step, in the direction that you wish to travel. It's like putting your creative process in gear so that it can move forward. An intention could be content based, like a goal: *I want to learn to meditate in order to better access my intuition;* or, if *I am creating a class/business, what is my curriculum?* Or, it could be in the form of a request: *Show me something I need to know for what is next.* Also, it might take the form of a prayer or affirmation: *I am open to receiving guidance for finding purpose in my life.* Through setting intention we begin to allow our creativity to manifest our reality.

When my divorce was final, I had to refinance and pay my ex for his share of the value of our home. I needed to stay in the home because my art business was licensed out of that location, and we had converted the garage into a studio. Also, my youngest son was still in high school. So moving could have proven difficult both due to school and licensure for a home business.

I had not wanted this house in the beginning; it was small for a family of five and had little storage. But we agreed to move in temporarily while we took time to find a home that would allow each of our sons to have his own bedroom and had a space that could be converted into an art studio. It didn't happen, and now I felt stuck, unable

Woman Alone: One Woman's Journey Through the Murky and Magical was published in 2018.

to make a move. I felt resentful. However, I also realized a new home might not allow for a home business, and I was "grandfathered in" at this location. At least this house was affordable and already had studio space. I knew that I needed to make the most of it. I needed to, little by little, as I could afford, make this home "me."

It has been a long process, but now I can't imagine being anywhere else. I have two studios, one for classes and one for creating my own art. I have a beautiful Zen Garden with inviting sitting areas on four levels of decking. I have a pond, a creek, and lots of trees. The best part of all—I created it.

I made the choice to make this my space. I set this as my vision. In some cases, circumstances arose that allowed me to create more than I thought I could afford. At one point friends asked to borrow three large paintings to stage a home they were displaying for sale. When a second house they were selling sold first, they determined to keep the first house. A week or so after returning the paintings to me, they called to say they wanted to purchase all three. "The house just isn't the same without your paintings," they said. I suggested we barter some construction work for the artwork. It benefited all of us.

I set an intention to work, project by project, toward making this house fit my needs perfectly, and things have flowed toward making that happen. It continues to be a living, changing project, and a nurturing, sacred space that renews and inspires me as well as my friends and family. There are also many wonderful stories that go with the creation of this space that served as signs that validated and inspired me.

A few years after the divorce, I was on a more stable financial footing and decided to update the kitchen. The cabinets were original and cheap. A few years earlier I had primed and painted them off-white, but they were now scratched and outdated. I started looking for what sort of cabinets I might like, took measurements, and got estimates. I came home one day, after a month of looking, feeling there was no way I would ever afford new cabinets. I sat down at my dining table and cried. Less than a month later I was at Home Quarters to pick up some paint for the studio and noticed "Going Out of Business" signs. All their kitchen displays were on clearance. I really liked the cabinets in one display, and although the layout was totally unlike my kitchen, I

Above: My fairy garden created in honor or my Mom.

Below: The view from my garden studio where I paint.

17

could envision changing things around, using a couple of overhead cabinets with the base and making it work. The total cost, considering a friend doing the plumbing for free and keeping the same countertops, was under $5000. Even the installers could not believe how I had imagined the fit.

Later, I was ready to finish the project by adding new countertops and removing a wall between the kitchen and dining area. I wanted to open this up so that I could install a nice large island. I needed the extra counter space. I could manage without additional cabinets, but the estimates were scary. My son Jeremy and his wife were looking for a new refrigerator. I was with them in an appliance store dreaming of a stainless, contemporary range hood, but the prices were high. A salesman came over to ask if I needed help. I told him what I was interested in, but added that I wasn't sure it was affordable.

"Would you be interested in the model we just took down from our display?" he asked. "It's in the back. The filters were lost in the process, but I'm sure you can order replacements. If you want it, you can have it for $100."

I followed him to the back where he pulled down a large box containing a beautiful Jenn Air contemporary range hood. I bought it on the spot. The stainless steel filters cost me another $60 from Jenn Air. I found the exact model online for $2700. This was my sign to say "go" on finishing the kitchen remodel.

I hired a young contractor to do the work. His was the lowest bid. In the process of remodeling he observed me working on a large painting in my garden studio where he stored his tools overnight. As he was working, I walked by on my way down the hallway and he said, "Jan, I absolutely love that painting you are working on. I know I could never afford it, but the cardinal in it makes me feel as if my grandmother is watching over me. She and I were very close and she loved cardinals."

As the project continued I thought about his comments and wondered if he might choose to purchase the painting if I hired him for another project. I needed some work done on the downstairs bathroom, and I might afford it if he purchased the painting. So, I asked him if he was serious about the painting. I said, if he was, I thought

The Garden Goddess

Meaningful art, enduring art—and the transformative process it awakens—keeps us alive.

Mark Nepo
(Drinking from the River of Light)

we might work something out. He was thrilled to make the deal. And as a result I got a most wonderful enlarged bathroom with beautiful tile, granite countertop, and a huge walk-in shower. I already had drawings of the design, as I was in the process of envisioning the means to make it happen.

The internet is filled with articles and the library with books that tell you how to set intentions. The important thing is to find what works for you. For some this is most readily achieved by walking or jogging. For some it works to sit in nature and simply soften the eyes and stare. Meditation works for others. I will share the process I use for myself and hundreds of clients. If it doesn't work for you, then please search sources for what will work.

Relaxation/Visualization Technique

1) The key to setting intentions is to relax so that you can enter the zone or the gap. I use a guided relaxation for this purpose: (A) Sit comfortably with eyes closed and begin with deep breathing. (B) As you become relaxed into your breathing, notice your feet and toes. With a deep breath in, tense and stretch them, then relax as you breathe out, consciously releasing any tension. Work your way up your body by next noticing the calves of your legs, tense them, then relax as you breathe out any tension. (C) Continue to your knees, thighs, chest, shoulders, elbows, hands, neck, etc., tensing then relaxing as you breathe out releasing. (D) Now focus on your face. Inhale, then breath out tension in the forehead, around the eyes, cheeks, and lips. (E) Next, let go of thoughts, desires, and all externals as much as possible. Allow your mind to be as clear and as relaxed as you can manage. It will get easier with practice. (F) Once you feel relaxed, count backward from 10 relaxing more deeply into yourself with each number. When you have reached zero, simply breathe slowly and deeply and be still. Allow whatever time you need to enter into a receptive state of mind.

Sit in the silence, be present, and listen. (insert period after listen). For it is in the stillness of an open heart that God can be heard.

The Garden Studio

2) Now, listen (10 to 15 minutes). By listening I mean to notice any calm thoughts, impressions, urgings that come to you. True guidance comes in a still, small voice.

3) When you feel ready, count back from zero to 10 bringing your consciousness slowly back to the present. Now, journal your experience. I like to write out my intention or intentions, then put them in a special place.

4) Finally, turn it over to God, the Universe, the Divine (however you think of that Higher Power).

5) Believe it will be manifested.

6) Take action as you are intuitively led. This means trusting that the calm thoughts, impressions, and urgings you receive are guidance from your Inner or Higher Self.

This procedure may feel awkward at first, but with practice, I assure you, you will have positive results.

Leaves

Flooding Fields, 24x36, oil and cold wax on canvas

We are constantly creating with every choice and every thought. The key is to learn to become so aware of your own personal power that you are creating with conscious intention rather than chaos.

Part Four

Plugging Into Your Power Potential

Learning to set healthy boundaries is a magically freeing experience. It is, also, a prerequisite for optimization of your personal power.

Photo by Fiani Osborne-Jackson

A boundary is a limit or space between you and the other person; a clear place where you begin and the other person ends. The purpose of setting a healthy boundary is, of course, to protect and take good care of you. Showing kindness and compassion for yourself is at the core of healthy boundaries. But the irony is that your healthy boundaries are also best for those who try to take advantage of your niceness. Mentally healthy people take responsibility for themselves. Enabling another means you are taking responsibility for what is actually that person's responsibility.

Authentic or personal power stems from the Authentic Self. The better you know your true self, the more your confidence grows, and the more authentic you become. This enables conscious choices and the setting of powerful intentions. This is why it is so important to practice "seeing" and "listening" to your teachers (all persons and experiences). It is by this kind of introspective seeing that you come to know your Self. I capitalize self here to emphasize this authentic, powerful Self from the self that gets caught up in fear. This authentic, Higher Self speaks in a calm, fearless voice, never clamoring or desperate. You must learn to calm the self and still the mind in order to hear this Higher Self. This is why meditation and contemplation are such important and powerful practices. You are simply calming that worried, fearful, little-self that Buddhists so appropriately call the "monkey mind."

I am a long-time practitioner of meditation, but it didn't come easy for me. I had to learn first to simply sit, breathe, and watch my thoughts. I learned it best not to fight those thoughts, but also to attempt not to hook on to one. Just let the thoughts flow on through. Gradually I learned to let go rather quickly and easily so that I could enter the "zone." I find it helpful to focus, with eyes closed, to the inside center of my forehead (the area called the third or Inner Eye). This allows me, with time, to enter an alpha brain state in which I see pulsating colors. Not everyone sees these colors, but it is at this point I know I am in a stilled, receptive state.

Finding your Authentic Self, and thus your personal power, requires getting to know yourself really well. No more pretending or hiding. You become much more comfortable with being uncomfortable. You also recognize the boundaries between yourself and others. You can let go (and say no) to "fixing" things for everyone else. You allow others to take responsibility for what is theirs to fix. No more codependency. As a result of this, you can now surround yourself with quality people who are able to mutually inspire and support you. You will be able to speak up when you need to, while at the same time not taking other people's issues personally. You realize that everyone is on their own journey, which means they have to learn from their own experiences, and you can stop trying to force them to avoid making mistakes. This is a very freeing place to be.

Many people struggle with boundaries. I found them very difficult. As a child my parents had conflicts over religion, and I took on the role of "little miss fix it" at a very young age. I would feel a knot build in my solar plexus when they were disagreeing and would do my best to find ways to make them happy and get them smiling. If the argument escalated, eventually Dad would become silent and stop speaking to Mom, sometimes for more than a day. This created tension for me and ramped up my need to make them happy. As a result, I developed a codependent nature, becoming the caregiver, the peacemaker in all sorts of situations.

You wouldn't believe how hard I worked to fix my marriage. And if someone didn't like me for whatever reason, I worked hard to change that as well. My religion had taught me to turn the other cheek, give beyond what was asked for, and forgive seventy-times-seven. But of course, you cannot make peace on behalf of others. They must take responsibility for their own choices. What a relief when finally I realized boundary setting is healthier for all concerned. Otherwise I was enabling others to keep blaming and avoiding problems only they could change.

A key for me in realizing I needed to set boundaries was when I began to feel resentment from giving too much. Resentment is a red flag reminding you to back off, to let go, and to stop taking responsibility for another's choices. You cannot access your Authentic Power without boundaries, but great personal power can result from healthy boundaries.

One valuable lesson in boundaries came through divorce; another came through learning to let go of the responsibility of keeping my diabetic son alive. Both were very difficult experiences, but amazing teachers concerning boundary setting.

My now ex-husband kept breaching my boundaries by involving me in a love triangle, which made it clear I had to choose divorce. I was so caught up in "saving my marriage" by trying to change my husband, I forgot I could only change myself and only make choices for myself.

For the first several years of his life, I literally kept my diabetic son alive. The time came when he needed to assume that responsibility for himself. Had I not set boundaries concerning what I would do for him, requiring that he take responsibility for his own food choices and medical care, he would not have learned to become independent and take care of himself.

The Authentic Self takes responsibility for its situations and its choices and sets healthy boundaries with others.

Sculpture by Niki de Saint Phalle

There is nothing more freeing than setting healthy boundaries!

What you allow is what will continue.

Unknown

Sun Kissed, 20x24, mixed media (collection of Bruce and Maryann Lucas)

Temptation

His words

Like the notes of a flute on the mountain

Vibrate in my bones.

His word music moves me into fantasy,

Fills me with longing for a joining that

Might make me whole.

But I have lived long on this mountain,

Content now in my own poetry,

Reluctant to allow another's song to

Carry me away from a peace that

Resides within.

My forty-three-year-old Bradford Pear tree.

I have come to understand that creativity is a spiritual portal of healing.

Part Five

Creative Energy is Healing Energy

At the deepest level the healing process and the creative process arise from the same source. You are artist, creator, and healer.

My Front Studio entry

Over several years I have created a garden that is ever growing and changing. On one particular morning after breakfast, while in the process of writing this book, I walked through the garden to my garden studio. I was contemplating a question: How does creativity or creative expression give me a fullness of life? I was greeted by yellow and orange day lilies, brilliant red cannas, and waving elephant ears among the myriad greens. The day lilies reminded me of my childhood as they were everywhere around our home, including the old abandoned houses scattered over our farm. They also reminded me of the wonderful old house on five acres my ex and I rented in Benton, Illinois, where we were able to also keep our horses. The cannas, which I had intended to add to the garden the year before, because they remind me of those my mom once grew in a large side garden, were a gift this spring from my nephew who also gave me the elephant ears. He didn't know of my intention. All good and positive memories were being stirred. I was surrounded by color, movement, and energy—such vibrant life! I walked into the cool studio to journal. Gratitude welled up inside me. My garden reminded me of the fullness of my life!

I had created this garden from intention, presence, and love. It was to be hot on this day, but the garden afforded a shady, breezy spot where I would share dinner with a friend later that evening. We would watch the sunset, listen to music, and share the events of our week. Again, I felt a fountain of gratitude.

The Bradford pear tree is responsible for much of the shade in my garden. It stands tall and happy, but it was wounded when it lost a limb this spring. I researched how to care for the tree, washed the wound with warm water and soap, and each time I passed by it I touched the wound with healing intention. Last time the Bradford lost a limb (it has lost a few over the years) I was told by an arborist that it had lived beyond its years and had to come down. The tree was twenty-eight then. Now it is forty-three. This Bradford pear also survived Fire Blight; another arborist had told me it could not. But it just keeps hanging on. I talk to this tree, I hug it, I remind it that it is integral to me and to the garden. I love that tree. And I believe it cares for me. When this limb fell, it fell so that the main weight of it landed directly centered on a beam post; it did no damage. Yes, it could have been a coincidence. But I believe my own creative energy affects this tree and its energy affects me.

Recently there have been many articles published on the amazing benefits of soaking up the energy of trees. Very popular in Japan, this is known as "forest bathing." Scientists have even learned that trees communicate. For example, in order to discourage herds of giraffes from eating their leaves, some trees in Africa release a scent mimicking the smell of a lion. We are learning much about the consciousness of trees.

I could tell so many stories of this garden and how I am nurtured and healed by its energy as it is also nurtured and healed by my love and tending. Nature inspires much of my creativity because of its relationship to creative, healing energy.

We come to love what we place focused attention on, whether nature or humans, and the energy we share through that loving focus heals both us and those we pour that loving energy out upon. I believe love is the most powerful creative energy. We heal and are healed by what we love.

We know, too, that creative energy is healing energy through the successes of music therapy, art therapy, poetry, and even crafts. By using this creative process in my years of teaching, I have seen people heal, grow stronger and more confident—even enough to make major life changes . We also now have scientific proof that the creative process releases the same feel-good endorphins in humans as physical exercise.

Bradford Pear Blooms, photograph by Stan Chambers

Our brains love novelty. For this reason creativity also brings satisfaction as we solve the varied challenges life brings. Sometimes we sustain physical injuries and other times those injuries are psychological. Either type of injury can leave us feeling disengaged from life, unwell, and powerless. When we acknowledge that we are always responding creatively as we find new ways to cope, our sense of purpose improves. We are constantly creating new ways to do things, whether we realize it or not. We are empowered, not powerless. The more we recognize and celebrate this everyday creativity, the more sense of satisfaction we find.

Even when we take a walk along a familiar trail, we are creating new experiences of that trail: how white the top of the sycamore is against the grays of winter woods and sky; how red the flitting cardinal appears as it flies against a summer-green landscape. These new experiences inspire and uplift us, which can result in an interesting journal entry, if not a poem, painting, or song. These daily creative experiences also serve to heal us, to make us "feel better." Remember how good you felt after that walk.

I once introduced the power of connecting with creative energy to new students by saying, "I am not responsible if you leave your wife or husband, or make other dramatic life changes. I'm simply teaching you a new way of seeing your world." Everyone would laugh, but in truth, I have seen students make life-changing decisions: divorce an abusive spouse or quit an engineering job to write a novel, etc., because they learned to "see" their world with fresh, creative eyes.

Being present in the moment and "seeing as an artist" are key factors in everyday creativity and healing. Be there, be awake, and see the miracles all around you, as Fredrick Franck wrote in *The Zen of Seeing*.

...to stop rushing around, to sit quietly on the grass, to switch off the world and come back to the earth, to allow the eye to see a willow, a bush, a cloud, a leaf, is an unforgettable experience.

Frederick Franck

I know artists whose medium is life itself, and who express the inexpressible without brush, pencil, chisel or guitar. They neither paint nor dance. Their medium is Being. Whatever their hand touches has increased life. They are the artists of being alive.

Frederick Franck

White Water Moon, mixed media 30x40

Bear Lake

We hiked Bear Lake then

Took the turn North

Toward that lonely, secluded pond,

Smelling of cracked mud—

A dried-up disappointment

Like the love lingering between us.

"Watch for Bear"

The signs warned

As we climbed switchback trails

Scattered with wildflowers:

Yellow, violet, blue, and boulders

That gave a sun-soaked invitation,

A warm welcome to be silent and

Listen for those that watched

Or sang us on our ascent.

We could almost believe,

In this magical wildness,

That we belonged,

That wounds and baggage

And fears could not defeat us.

But traveling home,

Back to city noise and smog,

We sensed a resuming reality

And the rising smell

Of endings.

Frog on Lily Pad

Tell me, what does it look like? This life that is everything you want?

Part Six

What Do You Want to Create?

Whatever else you do, create from your uniquely beautiful, Authentic Self. Be true to who you are.

In these next sections I want to share with you some possibilities for creating a life that is nurturing, inspiring, and meaningful. Of course, what constitutes these things for each person is varied; but my hope is that by sharing some of the ways I have created such a life, you will have your own ideas inspired and begin to form a vision that is uniquely you.

I have shared how after divorce I needed to move on by creating a space that fit with a vision for my own life as a mid-life, single, creative artist. That was just a beginning; I also had to reinvent myself on several other levels. I wanted a career as an artist that allowed me to make a living while I transformed my space and helped my youngest son get through a very difficult time. I wanted to continue making and marketing my art while teaching art classes out of my home studio, but to do so, I had to increase my income substantially.

Through the Inner Eye: Awakening to the Creative Spirit was published the same year my divorce was final. While writing that manuscript, I actually wondered if people would take the philosophy I was presenting seriously, as I had actually lived a pretty easy life compared to many. Yet, between the time the manuscript was finished and the book was published, I found myself living through a total "falling-apart-of-my-world." I believed in "happily ever after." I never intended to be divorced, and more than this, I thought I was in a good marriage, certainly a better-than-most marriage. It was a rude awakening. Words and concepts are nice, but living them is a different matter. There were times I felt lost. But there were also times I recalled the words I had written in my manuscript. I struggled to live my own words of wisdom. It was not easy, but I made it through, and I learned many lessons along the way.

Victoria Visitor Centre, Victoria, Canada

Through the Inner Eye: Awakening to the Creative Spirit proved to be a wonderful tool for expanding my workshops on creativity and personal growth, enabling me to increase my income. Being an author also gave me stronger credentials for drawing more art students. My vision for this new career was to market my workshops throughout the country, doing exhibits when possible in the locations where workshops were held. I thought about pursuing a Masters, but I wasn't sure I could spare the money or the time to make that happen. However, it was there, in the back of my mind, as an ideal part of my vision.

Note: When forming a vision, put down your dreams as well. Don't limit your possibilities.

One morning I got a call from Dr. Elaine Tillinger, the head of the art department at Lindenwood University. I didn't know Elaine, but she knew of me through Sandra, a former student of mine, who had just finished her Masters and was now teaching ceramics at the university. Sandra had suggested that Dr. Tillinger call me and discuss the possibility of me working on a Masters there. She was hoping I might end up teaching in the art department as well. Elaine literally convinced me to come in for a talk with her. It was as if something was manifesting from the back of my mind, even before I felt ready.

Ellaine said to me, "Jan, Sandra and I think you should come and work on your M.A. here. You are already a successful artist and author, and you can get several credits for your accomplishments and the book you've just published. What do you think?"

I nervously chuckled and said, "If you can tell me how to enter a graduate program without the time or money I will consider it."

"Well, I believe where there is a will there is always a way," Elaine replied, "and I will help you in any way I can."

After much thought, I made the decision to go for it. With the help of a scholarship and a grant, as well as credits toward the degree for my professional accomplishments, I was on my way. It was a challenge to be working full time, taking care of a home and gardens, and going to graduate school. But I loved it. A few times I had to cancel my private classes in order to get a paper completed on time. But in the end, it was an exciting accomplishment for me. I graduated with my family surrounding me the summer of 1997, the same time Lindenwood granted the famous baseball Cardinal, Ozzie Smith, an honorary degree! Now I had an advanced degree to add to my credentials, which made marketing workshops easier. The icing on the cake was that within a few months of my graduation I received a call from Dr. Michael Castro, asking if I would be interested in teaching a humanities cluster for the Lindenwood College of Individualized Education (LCIE). This was something I'd never considered. But I went for the interview with Dr. Castro and was hired as Adjunct Professor of Humanities, a position teaching Art History, World Literature, and Philosophy. It proved to be tailor made for me!

Art from nature.

More than one student, upon completing my humanities cluster, expressed how the class literally expanded their minds and changed their lives.

I hope you can see how setting a vision and intention for a sustaining career in the arts began a flow that took me in directions I could not have imagined when I initially set that vision. As the creative process took on a life of its own, I ended up with a wonderfully adventurous career traveling to facilitate workshops and doing art exhibits plus in-depth explorations of all areas of the humanities with my college students. All of this by remaining flexible and open to what might be drawn to me.

Canna, photo by Jan Groenemann

My art was represented in galleries from Florida to Lajolla, California, Scottsdale and Prescott in Arizona, and Atlanta, Georgia, as well as here in the Midwest. I became a Resident Artist at the Foundry Arts Centre in St. Charles, Missouri for five years, and was chosen as the artist to participate in a cultural exchange with St. Charles' sister city in Ludwigsburg, Germany, with the opportunity for two exhibits there. I met a musician/writer from San Diego and helped bring his musical, "Love at Any Age," to the St. Peters Cultural Arts Centre and acted as his assistant director in the production. That same year I won the St. Charles County Arty Award for Individual Accomplishment in the Arts. In addition, my art classes were full, and I had a waiting list. I was doing what I loved and being very successful at it!

Magic Carpet, photo by Jan Groenemann

It was after I built the Garden Studio and moved from the Foundry Studio that I began a deeper spiritual practice. I offered more creativity and life coaching, and I decided to enroll in a training program with the Institute for Life Coach Training. For quite some time another book had been forming in my head. I had started to write a few times, but it was when I was invited to join a writer's group that I began seriously working on my first novel, *Woman Alone: One Woman's Journey through the Murky and Magical.*

It was here, two years after *Woman Alone's* release, back in my home studios, slowly cutting back on classes so that I could do more coaching and creating (and just maybe semi-retire) that COVID-19 struck. My classes were stopped short. Book signings and promotional travel came to a halt. I wondered if it was time for me to retire. I decluttered, rebuilt my pergola, and repaired the decks, but it was not going to be time for me to retire.

My daughter-in-law, Renee, had decided to take a training program to learn how to take her business online, and she wanted me to join her. I was learning to do some classes via Zoom while isolating from the virus; maybe I could learn to create webinars and video shorts. I certainly had the material and a lot of workshop experience. Renee and I had talked about working together for some time and had even done a few workshops together. So here I am, writing *Creativity as a Life Path,* so that it can be a part of our online offerings! With flexibility life continues to be an adventure.

You, too, can create a work you love—even more than you might initially imagine! Just form that vision and set those intentions that move you toward it, then get your "self" (little self) out of the way and unleash your co-creating Authentic Self!

What is it you want your life to look like from this point on? What is working that you want to keep? What isn't working that you need to let go of? What are your dreams? What is your vision? You have the power potential! Just go for it!

Another area in which I have created a new vision is my spiritual life. I grew up in a very fundamental Christian belief system. My ex and I, throughout our marriage, had been very active in a church. This included being members of a very evangelical group in Benton, Illinois, that believed we should go door to door "selling" the idea of the gospel. I was uncomfortable with this, but I participated. I still remember the surprised looks on the faces of some of the people who were gracious enough to welcome us in, hear us out, and kindly thank us. When we moved back to the St. Louis area my spiritual seeking took on a new direction. I began to read voraciously from Martin Buber, Soren Kierkegaard, Thomas Merton, Thomas Moore, and many other spiritual writers. Something was missing for me in the fundamentalist approach I had been raised to follow. I had always been a seeker and one who questioned. Little by little I was led into what for me is a larger concept of God. My ex and I moved from the Christian church to an Episcopal church and then to a United Church of Christ that he had attended growing up. We were opening up, becoming more liberal. I share this to say I was aware that I was on a spiritual journey and that it tied in with my creativity. The messages I got from a painting I was working on were more often than not, spiritual messages— messages that pointed me to the next step on my journey.

Tree Wound

Creating sacred spaces in the garden for relaxation and renewal is a favorite project of mine.

Even as a young child I carried on daily conversations with God. At about ten I had an experience while watching a moonrise from my bedroom window—my first mystical experience. I heard the message as: God is not "out there," but "within." And, not just within me, but within *everything*.

After I divorced, I attended a few other churches, trying to find where I fit, but nothing seemed right. After my garden studio was built, and I moved back from the Foundry to that new space, I set a vision for a new spiritual practice. Instead of a church service, it would be a morning ritual of communing with nature and listening to Spirit through meditation and journaling. In sharing this, I am reminded of a book by Thomas Moore titled, *A Religion of One's Own*. That was what I determined to create for myself. It continues to be a wonderful and insightful journey for me through which I have explored Buddhism and Shamanism as well as deeper levels of contemplative Christianity. A discussion group that I organized a few years ago, "Spirit Walkers," has become a loving community in which to explore my spirituality.

I've written about creating a nurturing, sacred space and creating a work you love—but there is so much more to life. There are mutually supportive relationships to build, partnerships to form, and teams to join. Nothing else grows us quite like relating to others. From the patience required to the love that blossoms, there is nothing quite like relationship with the other. Here we find our greatest challenges and our deepest intimacies.

I enjoy my friendships. I draw to me inspiring, nurturing, supportive friends who have my back. As an introvert I require a good deal of solitude, but my friendships are a top priority to me. I believe it is important to put time and presence into your friendships. I have friends that I meet with on a regular basis, as in weekly or bi-weekly. Four of my close friends live at a distance now, but we still stay in close contact. I have a larger group that I see at least monthly. These include the members of my writer's group, Spirit Walkers discussion group, The Tribe (a support group made up mostly of fellow artists) and the TWOs (an acronym for The Weird Ones, meaning we like to discuss subjects too far out for many). The friends in these groups play a very important role in my life. I am ever grateful for what each of these groups, and the individuals within them, contribute to my quality of life as well as my personal and spiritual growth. My students have also become dear friends.

In addition to my company of friends, I treasure so deeply the relationships I have with my three sons, two daughters-in-law, and two grandsons. We are a family that can sit and talk about any subject, and I do know this is rare. We even enjoy family vacations together! They are the ones I know will always be there when I need them, even when I'm on my deathbed. And, yes, I am always there for them as well.

Relationships thrive with tender, loving, creative care. Don't forget to include how you want them to be in your vision.

As you can see, I have life-long, unconditionally loving, amazing friends! Where I find I struggle is with romantic relationships. As an empath, I see deeply into the souls of others finding any good that is there and magnifying it so that it overshadows anything not so good. I have been lovingly called "Suzy sunshine with rose-colored glasses." I do believe in the good that I see. It is there. But in my romantic love relationships, it has taken me a very long time to accept that actions, or follow through, are what I must judge to determine if I should let another person into my intimate space. Let me say that again, ACTIONS and BEHAVIORS, not WORDS over a period of time, need to be my basis for discernment. I have learned to take note of the "red flags." I've read many articles about people like myself. We have a gift. But we are also easily taken advantage of in love relationships, and narcissists are drawn to us.

I have no regrets, for I have learned much and had wonderful experiences in each relationship I have explored. They just haven't always turned out as I might have hoped. I have learned to better trust my intuition. In hindsight, my intuition has always been right, and I could have saved myself a lot of energy and more than a few tears to have acted on that first gut instinct that "something isn't quite right with this situation." But I was taught that we are to forgive seventy-times-seven, right? I have learned to apply this forgiveness to myself as well.

My creative daughter-in-law, Meaghan. You can see why she always wins first place in the equine Halloween costume contest.

Leave time for reading and introspection.

Don't forget to create time to keep your body and mind in good health. I love walking in nature. Walking is also a good time to let your mind get into the creative zone.

After my divorce, I was feeling very rejected and abandoned, so I set an intention that I would not get involved with a man unless he pursued me, and wined and dined with roses and chocolates. I drew a man to me who knew the romance angle. There was chemistry, fun, and romance. He also had a love for the arts. You couldn't do the kind of art he was doing unless you were connecting in that zone. And all that self-confidence! It wasn't ego--right?

Without going into details, I'll just say, my next intention was not to get involved with a man unless he took his time, moved slowly, and let me get to know him without being pushy. I drew a man who fit these exact criteria. It took him weeks to ask me out! Then, it was weeks before he kissed me. You get the idea. I almost married this man. But circumstances caused us to decide to move in together first, and everything changed. We were both unhappy, and not totally sure why. After a few therapy sessions, we decided to go our separate ways.

Now I knew I needed the romance and the chemistry, but I also needed lots of time to really get to know someone. Yes, I drew just such a man. Exciting, romantic, intellectual, creative, fun, and what chemistry we had. I fell hard. It took a long time to realize he wasn't exactly a fan of the truth. Enough said.

I am yet to find that "right" partner, or could it be that each relationship was "right" for what we each had to learn at the time? I do know each relationship was a growth experience for me; I certainly grew to understand myself better.

There are guidelines I have learned to apply. Trust that strong gut feeling you have! Know that being lied to is never okay. When it doesn't feel right, it isn't right. When you aren't being nurtured, cared for, inspired, respected, and supported then it isn't the "right" relationship. Trust your intuition, not chemistry.

I am very good at creating and guiding others to do the same. I can manifest amazing things. But a romantic relationship is one area where I have yet to achieve the success I desire. I am still learning. Even great manifesters can be wrong!

All humor aside (and it is important to be able to laugh at yourself), I'd like to share with you in this final section how I help my coaching clients to begin their journey of conscious creating. *It's time for you to do your work.*

As you can see, creating the life you want, a life you love, includes addressing every aspect of your existence. The life I love creating includes the little things as well as the big things. It includes putting together a grouping of significant objects on the top of a dresser or night stand. It includes collecting items that are symbolic for me (rocks, books, driftwood, small art pieces I've brought home from special places I've visited, intimate gifts from special people in my life, and art I love from other artists). It is creating inviting garden rooms in my garden space and displaying my own art in my home and studio spaces. Also included is music I love, a vase of flowers for students to draw, incense, chimes, so many small things that add just that special touch that says I treasure you. I call these small things "soul food," and the challenge is to fill your space with those inspiring, nurturing touches without it getting cluttered.

On my deck I have created a fairy garden that daily reminds me of my mom who loved dolls, miniature houses, and furniture. My fairy garden has a koi pond, a bridge, a fairy boy fishing, a fairy girl playing the flute, an artist fairy. It also is filled with colorful flowers and my herbs that I like to add to foods. It is a place where I think of Mom, and it brings joy both to me and friends who visit.

In the far back corner of my yard, nestled between two huge southern pine trees, I have, with the help of my grandsons, created a healing circle with small stones. Here I love to lay out my yoga mat and lie on my back gazing up into the tree tops. My grandsons like to join me here as well. It's a wonderful place for staring up into the trees and soaking up their good energy. Here is also a hanging screen made from corkscrew willow twigs (from the trees in my yard), pieces of leather, ribbon, and yarn. It gives a bit more privacy from my neighbor and carries an interesting energy of its own. I also have a totem pole there that my sons and I created from the remains of a third pine tree that died years ago. We wrapped it in copper that we tooled with creatures and designs, bits of copper wire bent into spirals and circles, wire-wrapped stones, and assorted treasures. It is topped by a copper cone.

These fun, creative surprises are scattered throughout my very modest quarter-acre suburban property. Each has special meaning, each reminds me to be present, to live the now, to be grateful. Even my potting shed became a work of art with a painted black and white checkered floor, white walls, and fun garden quotes written all over the walls. Think about how you can make your space more soulful, and remember, the fun is in the details.

Relationships thrive with tender, loving, creative care. Don't forget to include how prominently you want them to figure in your vision.

Creating a life you love includes paying attention to the details. Putting yourself and a lot of energy into all that you love: your spaces, your work, and your relationships. Every morning I awake with "thank you, thank you, thank you" in my heart.

Creating special memories with family.

Each student who has come for private art classes will tell you it took effort to take that first step. When I discontinued most of my classes the group of women above continued to meet, and I with them, as what we have coined "The Tribe."

There is an intuitive leap of faith required to create. You must take that first step into the unknown.

Part Seven

Getting Started

Have you ever watched a bird take flight? It must take that leap of faith, that small jump, trusting fully that its wings will work.

Hopefully by this point you are beginning to believe that you are a creator, and that you are co-creating constantly with the guidance of a Higher Power. What you think, how you act, and choices you make—these are powerful tools that are important to use with intention. Otherwise, you may create negative things and chaotic situations. You've heard, no doubt, the old adage: Be careful what you wish for. Don't be haphazard about what you visualize in your life. Make conscious and thoughtful choices and set conscious and thoughtful intentions. But whatever else you do, take the leap.

As a life coach, after getting to know my client through a rather lengthy questionnaire and first interview, I begin to work with my client on creating a vision. Your Vision is your foundation, your rock solid feet. My question: What is it you really want your life to look like from this point forward? Be specific. This question is so important, because you cannot create the life you want if you have no idea what you want. You don't just leap into the unknown. Create your Vision, see that Vision, make it as real in your mind as possible. Then you can let go and leap!

It is helpful to begin with three lists: (1) What is working in my life that I want to keep? (2) What isn't working in my life that I want to change? (3) What do I not have in my life that I want to add? From these three lists you can get a very good start on your vision.

The only way to create a new normal is to move outside your comfort zone and practice, practice, practice. It will be so worth it!

Next, consider any hopes and dreams that you may have set aside or simply given up on. Is there something on that list that you want to reinstate in your life? Or is there something you have long dreamed of that you might be ready to actually act on? In this initial vision, reach for the sky. What have you always wanted your life to be but were afraid to even hope for it? I can't emphasize enough that *you must first have a vision.*

Go back, take another look at the "life balance wheel" and put your vision into written form. Let the above questions guide you as you begin. Let the sky be the limit. Do this now. This is your first step.

Photo to right by Meaghan Groenemann

Left: Sunset in Barcelona. Travel has often been a financial leap for me; but always I have been so rewarded.

Below: My youngest son took a leap outside his comfort zone to learn to ride; it gave him a whole new world of adventure, and some very special time with his horse-loving wife.

Ode to a Pond

Be sure when scheduling priorities to begin with what is most important rather than what is most stressful.

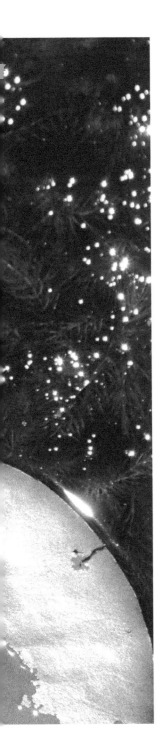

Part Eight

Prioritizing Your Presence

We need to give up what no longer works and find new ways of being that keep us close to what matters.

Mark Nepo (*The Book of Awakening*)

We have talked much about vision, so, obviously, before you prioritize your life, it is important to have a vision for it. You must know what is really important to you and where you are headed so that you can distinguish which activities are simply distractions and which activities are moving you toward your vision. Without a vision, prioritizing makes little sense. Consider vision in the way I have illustrated below: Having formed your vision, visualize it clearly in the upper right area of your mind. Now visualize your starting point in the lower left area. Intention follows a line that connects the two, with each step intended to move you forward and upward. Therefore, it is important to consider if each intention you set and each choice for action that you take moves you upward toward your vision. If not, why are you choosing it? Does it put you in a place better suited to move toward that vision? If not, then you need to reconsider and make a better choice.

Make a plan for how you will move toward and eventually reach the vision you want to become a reality for your life.

Sometimes the simplest and best use of our will is to drop it all and just walk out from under everything that is covering us, even if only for an hour or so—

Mark Nepo
(The Book of Awakening)

Cousins

VISION

n

o

i

CHOICES   t

n

e

t

n

i

YOU ARE HERE

It is also important to learn to say "No." This means saying no to what you are tempted to allow to distract you. You may be drawn to wander off your path toward your vision out of laziness or procrastination. You may convince yourself, "Ah, it won't matter if I eat two slices of this pie today. I'll be back on my intended healthy eating tomorrow." Or, "I'm not in the mood to write today; I'll start that novel tomorrow."

You also may have to say no to someone who is constantly distracting you from your vision by pulling you toward what they want, even though it conflicts with what you want in your life. You may be taking responsibility for someone with whom you are co-dependent, rather than being responsible for moving toward your vision.

Listen attentively both to others and to that still small voice within yourself. There are people who speak more and listen less—don't be one of them. Listening to things attentively can reduce the problem of distraction to a great extent. Listening helps you to know when a choice is right for you, or to recognize when someone else is manipulating you. Be more present in each moment, and stay connected to what is real. Be observant about your surroundings and work to stay emotionally balanced.

Being comfortable with your surrounding environment will also help you effectively prioritize and make healthy choices. I find it important to have creative and nurturing physical space in which to grow. A space that is uncluttered and gives me a view of nature inspires my creative expression. Music also helps me find calm and peace and allows for better hearing my inner guidance.

We have already discussed the importance of being comfortable within yourself enough to know what is best for you. Practicing yoga and meditation are two basic things that many find helpful in developing presence of mind. Yoga relaxes the body while at the same time connecting it with mind and Spirit. Meditation stills the mind so that you can connect with that "still small voice" that speaks from your Higher Self and Higher Power. I find that each of these helps me stay centered, provides mental calm that aids my ability to listen, and helps in the practice of being my Authentic Self.

When the sweet ache of being alive, lodged between who you are and who you will be, is awakened, befriend this moment. It will guide you. Its sweetness is what holds you. Its ache is what moves you on.

Mark Nepo
(The Endless Practice)

Keep in mind that you can't prioritize one thing and schedule another. Where you actually spend your time is where your values are. If you make it a priority to spend a certain amount of time with your family, and then schedule meetings that constantly conflict with family time, you have to accept that family *is not* the priority for you that you claim it to be.

Constantly consider "is this what I'm really meant to do? Is this what I really want?" You must be honest with yourself when setting priorities or you will always fail to live up to them, resulting in feelings of failure.

Another suggestion is don't go it alone. Find someone, a trusted friend, a life coach, a therapist, to hold you accountable for what you are saying are your priorities. This person can gently point out when your choices are taking you off track as well as cheer you on when you succeed.

In addition to prioritizing by using the Life Balance Wheel, it is helpful to prioritize tasks you must accomplish each day. Prioritizing tasks reduces stress and increases productivity. It also allows you more time for rest and relaxation. Knowing that you don't have to finish all tasks at once, or in a single day, will give you more flexible time to focus on the most important things first.

I suggest prioritizing as follows:

1) **Things most important to you** such as making time for those you love and are responsible for, fulfilling your job description responsibilities, and healthy self-care.

2) **Things that are urgent and pressing** such as crises and deadlines that must be met in order to take care of what is important.

3) **Things not so urgent, but still important** such as long- term planning, vacations, things you can set aside time to give attention to.

4) **Things that must be done, but are not your top priority**, i.e., unnecessary phone calls, returning some emails, some pointless meetings, mowing the lawn, cleaning the house, home maintenance (delegate as much of this as possible).

Do not let the urgent take precedence over the important.

Jayaraman Ramachandran

From Garic's Garden

Photo by Garic Groenemann

5) Trivial Matters (delete as many of these as you can). These may include playing computer games, being on the phone with friends, spending time at a bar after work, binge watching a series on TV.

Look deeply into what is *truly* important to you. Be fully committed to your priorities. Prioritizing family time then being on your phone for work while with family is *not* being present. Having a date night with your spouse and constantly checking text messages is *not* being present. Being present is giving focused attention to that person or project you have delegated as a priority at that moment in time.

Take some time now to write out your priorities and number them from most important to least important. Use the balance wheel to determine the percentage of your time you want to commit for each priority. *Be honest with yourself.*

Photo by Garic Groenemann

If you prioritize one thing then schedule another you aren't being honest with yourself.

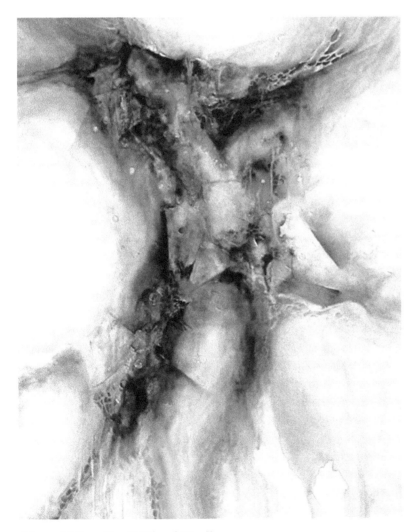

Alone At Sea, **3'x 4' Mixed Media**

Higher Perspective, 5'x6' mixed media (Collection of City of St. Peters)

Part Nine

Seeing from a Higher Perspective

We each deserve the freedom to perceive and create as a means of self-revelation. It is how we build self-confidence and come to know who we are on the deepest levels.

It seems that what we see too often depends on what we look for. No doubt this is true in our present day, over-politicized world. Often we see only what we want to see. And it follows, that when this is our perspective, we also tend to see in black and white and with tunnel vision. Saint Paul wrote about this in the New Testament as, "Now we see through a glass darkly." (First Corinthians 13:12 KJV)

The creative mind, however, sees in a very different way. The creative mind sees in possibilities. Those possibilities tend to include unity and equality fed by unconditional love. We rarely find more open-minded, tolerant, and accepting people than those in the creative areas of humanity. Think of the diversity of life on this planet, even the diversity in humanity. Do we really think this is an accident? Do we really believe that some of us are superior and others inferior? Are we inferior if we have brown eyes rather than blue, or red hair rather than black? How strange to categorize the value of a human by anything so shallow as the color of their skin, gender, sexual orientation, or any other physical characteristic. How shallow to judge anyone according to their cultural customs and behaviors. If we grew up in their culture we would most likely have a similar world view.

This past year I joined a group called "Important Conversations" (a part of Inner Eye Life Coaching) in which we have taken a long hard look at systemic racism through discussion and through reading the books *White Fragility, How to be an Anti-Racist, Between the World and Me,* and others. We have also watched movies such as "Thirteen" and "I Am Not Your Negro." We are a racially and culturally diverse group. For the first time I came to see just how much I have been enculturated to see white as superior without even realizing it and have benefited by that very same culture of inequality.

The world is full of endless possibility! We never know what may lie around the next corner.

Photo by Garic Groenemann

I challenge you to look long and hard at your perspective. I promise you, if you determine to be a thriving, growing, creative, spiritual being, your perspective will change. Change is the one sure thing (other than death) that we will experience in this human existence. I challenge you to change so that more and more you can view your life from a higher perspective that sees the beauty and possibilities in diversity. I challenge you to look upon this universe with eyes of love and watch the hate dissipate. Don't be afraid of change, welcome it. In the beautiful words of Gandhi, "Be the change you wish to see in the world."

If you are one who seeks to know yourself on deeper levels, thus to grow, I have no doubt you are on the path to this sort of change. When I look back upon my life, I am truly amazed by the many changes I have experienced, and I am still changing! I started out a sincere believer in a fundamentalist form of Christianity that harshly judged even other followers of the same Christ, believers in the same God. I was taught that unless you understood the scriptures as our denomination taught, you were wrong and in danger of hell.

By the grace of a Higher Power I have grown beyond such judgment and fear. I know the Divine is so much larger than our petty doctrines and feeble attempts to define and thus "box in" that which religions call God or Allah or any other name ascribed to that Higher Power. I am "absolutely sure" of less than I thought I knew then, but I am full with such a greater love for my fellow humans and for all that share this planet earth, and also the Universe. I wish to love and care for all. I see the sacred in every life form, even every stone. I think of another Biblical quote from Luke 19, "even the stones will cry out!" and I am in awe that through quantum physics we are learning that yes, that may be very true, that consciousness may exist in every particle.

How often do we see what we want to see rather than what is?

If we are all walking around with different, and often conflicting realities, then what is real?

I am humbled by the complexities and intricacies of this world. And I rejoice in being part of all that complexity as well.

**Photo by
Garic Groenemann**

First Time

Rounding the curve on Interstate 70,

Distance suddenly disappearing

Into mountain meadows,

A plinth of unrestrained color

Stretching, reaching, toward blue sky.

A catch of breath—

Nothing had prepared me for such

Sound of music, joyous

Twirling with arms toward the clouds, and

Escape of song from my throat,

Rocky Mountains high

Rain

My garden sings with her,

Sparkles as each drop splashes

Into the agitated pond where

Submarined Koi sit silently as if

Mesmerized by the rhythm.

Slowly one golden, blackened ship

Slips to the shining surface,

Sucking and sipping at each drop.

The low-toned taps on the roof continue—

All the rhapsodies of the rain-music,

Each playing its part in the symphony:

The high trickling sounds,

The sweeping sheets of sound,

Swelling to a crescendo.

A swoosh and a splash and a pour

As the gutter overflows onto the stones,

Then

The music slows, softens

As the rain stills.

Now just a drip,

Drip,

Drip.

Be Still and Know, 36x36, Oil and Mixed Media

Part Ten

Tools for Connecting

Everybody needs sacred space, a sense of place, connection with nature, and those things that nurture. Be sure you allow these for yourself.

Through the opened heart, the world comes rushing in, the way oceans fill the smallest hole along the shore. It is the quietest sort of miracle; by simply being who we are, the world will come to fill us.

Mark Nepo
(The Book of Awakening)

Your sacred space is where you can find yourself again and again.

Joseph Campbell

Some of the nature objects I've collected for my special space.

As you set out to find your creative life path I'd like to address some of the tools that can aid you in your journey. The first tool for creating the life you want is an open heart. So often we let others set our limits. Even our culture sets limits for us. You are an unlimited spirit whose nature is to create. Keep this foremost in your mind. You are creating with every thought and every choice, so if you are filled with limiting thoughts you will feel you have limited choices. Open your heart to the incredible Creative Spirit that is you.

I will summarize some of the best tools you have for opening yourself to your full creative potential. But first, I ask you to allow your mantra to be: "I am an unlimited creative being."

Now, begin to determine what the best consciously creative practice is for you. When can you carve out enough time in your day or week for utilizing these tools? For me it is early morning, but for some evening works best. Your natural rhythm as well as your schedule will determine what time is best for you. The ideal is a daily practice, of course, but if you are stretched for time begin with a weekly practice.

A SACRED SPACE

Next create a quiet place where you are unlikely to be interrupted. I love to go to my garden studio since it gives me a sense of leaving the house where dishes, laundry, or a to-do list, may distract me. Below are items I use to make my quiet place feel sacred:

- Candles signifying entering a meditative time. Be sure the scent and color is soothing to you, or use unscented if you are sensitive to smells.

- An altar with inspiring items I've collected. A photo of my altar is pictured to the right. I have collected stones, seed pods, bones, small meaningful gifts that were especially inspiring from important people in my life, sculptures, candles, nature objects, and art pieces.

- A place where I feel connected with nature. I am blessed to have a view of my garden and Koi pond from my garden studio. If you don't have an inspiring view then use photos or paintings to create that feeling for you.

- A beautiful journal and a pen you enjoy using: It is important to me that the journal and pen feel good in my hands.

- Music that inspires and soothes. I love classical such as Chopin, but I also like music designed for relaxation or meditation; there are also times I require silence.

- A book of daily readings that speak to me. I have used writings from various authors for my morning readings, but some of my favorites have been Mark Nepo's *Book of Awakening*, Wayne Dyer's *Wisdom of the Ages*, a series of small books called *Cherokee Wisdom*, several books of Zen quotes, and Mary Oliver's poetry.

- Incense. I find that soothing scents can be very effective. Experiment with what scents appeal to you.

- Fresh flowers. Their beauty helps to set the mood for connecting with your Inner Self. I have come to enjoy buying flowers for myself on a regular basis.

- Fresh air, when the weather permits. I find meditating outdoors or even throwing open the windows and doors adds to the ambiance of my special place. I like to hear the sound of the creek, the birds and my chimes.

- Chimes. If you don't have them I suggest you make them an addition.

- Soft sheer curtains. I often hang sheers from my pergola, which I can see and enjoy from my meditation space as they billow in a breeze.

The point is to make your own special, quiet space that speaks to your senses and contributes to your sense of beauty, solitude, and peace.

Artful Journaling is a very effective technique for inspiring creativity. It's also important to me that my journal is beautiful, and my pen feels good in my hands.

My altar, which is filled with objects from nature that I've collected; a Buddha sculpture that was a gift; a totem sculpture done by a dear friend; candles; incense, sage, cedar, stones from special places I've been; small totems that were gifts or special finds.

RELAXATION TECHNIQUE

- Sit in a comfortable position, but one in which you won't fall asleep. Close your eyes.

- Take long slow breaths, breathing in through the nose and out through the mouth. Notice any tension and breathe into that tension. Do this conscious breathing for ten breaths.

- Bring your attention to your toes and feet. As you breathe in stretch toes and feet. As you breathe out let go, relax feet.

- Repeat.

- Bring attention to your ankles. Stretch your ankles as you breathe in. Relax as you breathe out. Repeat.

- Now bring attention to your calves. Breathe in and stretch; breathe out and relax. Repeat.

- Move up to your thighs and breathe in as you tense thighs. Relax as you breathe out. Repeat.

- Now to the buttocks. Tighten as you breathe in, relax as you breathe out. Repeat.

- Now breathe in deeply, then hold as you tighten lower belly. Relax as you breathe out. Repeat.

- Breathe in deeply and hold as you tighten abdominal muscles. Relax as you breathe out. Repeat.

- Now upward to pectorals: breathing in, hold and tighten pecs; relax as you breathe out. Repeat.

- Move now to shoulders. Lift both shoulders to ears as you breathe in. Relax shoulders, then push down as you breathe out. Repeat.

- Drop chin to chest and as you breathe in roll head all the way around to right, then back to left as you breathe out. Repeat.

- Now consciously relax the muscles of the jaw, cheeks, around eyes and forehead as you slowly breathe in and out. Repeat until you feel your face is very relaxed.

- Now breathing as is comfortable, imagine with each breath you are filling your body with air until you are so light you begin to lift upward off the chair, through the ceiling, out into warm sunshine.

Your safe place should be a place where you can be at peace enough to forget the outward and go inward.

- Allow yourself to float away to a place where you feel safe. Settle into that place by sitting or laying in a position that is very comfortable for you.

- Relax as deeply as you can as you count slowly from 10 down to one, allowing yourself to sink more deeply into the chair or bed as you count.

- Now that you are relaxed, stay here for 10 minutes, or if you are doing a VISUALIZATION as well, begin that visualization.

VISUALIZATION

- Having reached this deeply relaxed state, look out upon the horizon and visualize a white fluffy cloud moving slowly toward you.

- Allow the cloud to come so close that you can touch it and smooth it out. Now allow your mind to see images on this cloud as on a screen.

- Ask for your Spirit Guide to join you (may be a person, animal, or whatever comes).

- Ask your Guide questions you have determined beforehand. Could be "What is my purpose here?" "What is the answer to the problem I am dealing with?" You can determine the questions after reading this book.

- Spend as much time with your Guide as you need. Follow your Guide wherever it takes you (a walk, a hike). Listen and remember.

- When ready, count back from 1-10, slowly allowing yourself to come back into the present where you will feel the weight of your body in the chair. You will slowly become aware of sounds, scents, and where you are.

- Open your eyes and write everything you can recall about the experience in your journal.

- You may receive more insights as you journal. Record those as well.

- Read back through your journal entry and add anything more that comes to you.

Journaling can take many forms. Above are more examples of Artful Journaling (using images as well as words).

NOTE: You can record these instructions for meditation and visualization so you have a verbal guide to help you relax.

Collections of special objects as above and fresh flowers, especially wild flowers, can add meaning to your special place.

- Use the RELAXATION and VISUALIZATION TECHNIQUES and make your list of questions that will help you determine your vision.

- Before you begin your RELAXATION review PART TWO.

- **Vision is the manner in which one sees or conceives of something**. It is a mental image produced by the imagination. We can say, vision is the ability or an instance of great perception, especially of future creations. It is the proven best strategy for creating a life you love. Think of vision as the bigger picture; it defines who you want to be, what you want to be known for, and the set of experiences and accomplishments you aim for. Vision sets the framework for choices and intentions.

- Using the Balance Wheel, write out your VISION for YOU.

- Make your list of questions to ask your Spirit Guide (your Higher Self).

- Now RELAX and VISUALIZE, then Journal.

CLEAR INTENTIONS

- **Intention is defined as a thing intended, an action or a plan.** An intention is similar to, but more flexible than, a goal, thus allowing for more creativity. In relationship to your vision, an intention is a step that takes you closer to that vision. Think of vision as what you are moving toward and intention as the movement on the path you are taking to get there.

- Review PART THREE on INTENTIONS.

- Make out your list of questions concerning steps to take to get to your VISION.

- Use RELAXATION and VISUALIZATION TECHNIQUES.

MEDITATION

- Opens one to connect with ones Higher Self
- Reduces stress and anxiety
- Promotes emotional health and self-awareness
- Lengthens attention span and improves memory
- Improves sleep and increases longevity

PRACTICE, PRACTICE, PRACTICE

- Purchase guided relaxation and visualization CDs (from Inner Eye Life Coaching or from other sources).
- The more you practice breathing techniques and relaxation techniques, the easier it becomes.
- You can also begin with a few sessions of coaching for learning these techniques.

REMEMBER

- You are creating every day with every choice you make. Learn to create consciously.
- The better you know yourself the better choices you will make for you.
- The more conscious you become the more intentional your creating.
- You want to make choices that take you closer to your VISION.
- If your choice takes you away from your VISION it is not a good choice for you.
- Your Higher Self has the right answers for you. This is how you connect with the DIVINE.

Bring in nature as much as you can: rock collections, seed pods, leaves, photos. and live flowers.

JOURNALING

- Opens one to inner guidance
- Reduces stress
- Boosts immune system
- Keeps memory sharp
- Boosts mood
- Strengthens emotional functions

Photograph taken over southwestern Canada

Free your imagination, for that is what determines how high you can fly!

Part Eleven

Time to Fly

Similar to a butterfly, I've gone through a metamorphosis, been released from my dark cocoon, embraced my wings, and soared!

Dana Arcuri

Our cows sometimes came to the barn on their own at milking time, but they never strapped on the milking machines.

Even an automatic transmission must be moved into forwarding gear.

Leaving the past behind

I grew up on a farm in southern Missouri milking cows, feeding chickens and pigs, hauling hay. So, of course, I grew up learning "delayed gratification," "getting the hard stuff out of the way first," "working hard so you could then enjoy playing hard." I love the quote about not waiting for the cow to back up to you before you could have milk. You must take the action; you must make the leap that gets your feet off the ground. No one can do it for you.

There is a song by REO Speedwagon that spoke to me clearly when everything was changing in my life and I felt fear and a need to hide away somewhere until all settled. *Time for Me to Fly* inspired me to fly rather than to hide away. And I just kept on flying. I've found I really love flying! I believe in the concepts I have shared with you. More than this, I have lived (and continue to live) these same concepts to the best of my ability.

Flying carries with it a sense of flowing with who you really are, allowing yourself to be lifted and carried by the winds of your own imagination. Flying entails living your passion and purpose with a sense of freedom and joy. Flying also means trusting that it takes the good along with the bad to create a truly full and balanced life.

For me, flying has meant everything and everyone is my teacher, and I learn and grow from each experience. I have learned to go with the flow, stop fearing change, and walk through every door. This moved me from that initial vision of teaching high school art and business until I could "make it as an artist," into Humanities Professor, accomplished painter, workshop facilitator, and author of three books, and soon to release a fourth.

In this process I have learned what matters to me in life and consciously made choices so that those really important things became my priorities. I have created sacred work that brings me joy and a sense of purpose. And, most of all, I have peace. At least once a year, I reassess my life and ask again: "What do you want your life to be from this point forward?" Because I am constantly changing, my vision changes. But always it is a beacon out there shining me toward heights that inspire me and allow me to soar more freely.

Now is the time for you to move toward the vision you have imagined, put it down in writing, commit to it, and begin living it out. Keep your eyes on that vision while remaining flexible when needed. With each choice ask, "Does this take me closer to my vision?" If so each step will lift you higher and higher until, finally, with one last leap, you will find that you, too, can fly.

If you are too afraid to leap, you will never fly. No one can fly for you!

Inside each of us is a wildish nature that we both fear and are called to express. Inside you is a song only you can sing, a poem only you can write—a life only you can live!

View from the southern coast of France

Contact Jan Groenemann and Inner Eye Life Coaching for information on our private one-on-one coaching, group coaching, online groups and programs, and Creativity and Coaching Intensives.

hokseda@charter.net, or www.jangroenemann.com, renee@spiritedgrowth.com

Go now and see all the beauty that is on this planet and in this Universe and know the beauty that is within your own wonderful creative Self. And as you go truly see and create a life you love.

About The Author

Jan Groenemann is a masterful and prolifically creative painter in mixed media who has won many awards and exhibited internationally. She is the author of two previous books: *Through the Inner Eye: Awaking to the Creative Spirit* and *Woman Alone: One Woman's Journey Through the Murky and Magical.* As a poet and mystic, a creator of sacred spaces, a teacher, and a life coach who nurtures creativity in others, Jan lives the message she shares in *Creativity as a Life Path*. Through the power of everyday creativity, she has created a life she loves, and in *Creativity as a Life Path,* she shares her wisdom so that you, too, can create the life you want.

Jan resides in St. Peters, Missouri where she paints in her garden studio overlooking her Japanese-inspired garden, coaches and hosts retreats in her front studio gallery, and is working on her fourth book, a second novel, "A Thousand Ways to Kiss the Earth." She is also creating a series of mixed-media paintings of this same title.

Jan is the mother of three sons, Jason, Garic, and Jeremy, has two beautiful daughters-in-law, Renee and Meaghan, and is Oma to two teen grandsons, Jaden and Skylar.

Groenemann Studios hosts monthly Spirit Walkers, a discussion group, The Tribe, an art and reading group, and a Writer's Group. These groups of creative and talented friends help Jan balance her need for creative solitude and her love for people.

Jan welcomes visitors by appointment to view her original art or to participate in her Creativity and Coaching Intensives.

You can contact Jan at: hokseda@charter.net or on her website at: www.jangroenemann.com

Lightning Source UK Ltd.
Milton Keynes UK
UKHW020232180223
417109UK00009B/159

9 798765 235324